THE TAO OF SILENCE

THE TAO OF SILENCE

Lo Po Hu

ASTROLOG PUBLISHERS

Astrolog Publishing House
P.O.Box 1123, Hod Hasharon 45111, Israel
TEL/FAX. 972-9-7412044
E-Mail: info@astrolog.co.il
Astrolog Web Site: www.astrolog.co.il

© Astrolog Publishing House 1998

ISBN 965-494-006-X

All rights reserved. No part of this publication may be reproduced, stored in a retrieval system, or transmitted, in any form or by any means, electronic, mechanical, photocopying, recording or otherwise, without the prior permission of the publisher.

Published by Astrolog Publishing House 1998

Distribution:
U.S.A & CANADA by APG - associated publishers group
U.K & EUROPE by DEEP BOOKS
EAST ASIA by CKK Ltd

Printed in Israel
10 9 8 7 6 5 4 3 2 1

The Tao Of Science

Who will teach me Tao?

The Tao Of Silence

The Tao Of Silence

Who will teach me silence?

The Tao Of Silence

The Tao Of Silence

The name Lo Po Hu, teacher of the Tao of Silence, appears already, in one way or another, in Chinese manuscripts from five thousand years ago.

In his later incarnation we find his name in the Tibetan Book of the Dead, in the Egyptian Book of Life, and in the Book of Essence, which forms the basis of Christianity.

Later incarnations of Lo Po Hu are not documented. Signs of the essential elements of his doctrine appear in the Jewish Kabbalah and in numerous philosophies of Islam.

In his present incarnation, Lo Po Hu has defined the principles of the Tao of Silence, gathered his proverbs, and published them in this modest book which is about to be published in dozens of languages throughout the world.

The Tao Of Science

The Tao Of Silence

The Tao Of Silence

The Tao Of Silence

The Silence Of The Tao

The Tao Of Silence

And the pupil asked:

What am I to do, my Master, in order to achieve the Tao of Silence?

The Master replied:

Firstly, do not trust in your own abilities, sublime as they may be.
Secondly, care not for anything which has already been thought or done and therefore belongs to the past.
Thirdly, control your tongue.
Fourth, restrain your stomach.

And the pupil listened.

The Tao Of Silence

And the pupil asked:

Why, Master, are there three benches for the pupils of the Tao of Silence?

The Master replied:

There are three kinds of pupils who come to study the Tao of Silence — those whose desire overcomes them and thus they seek to battle their desire; those who have overcome their desire and they seek to enable all people to overcome their desire; and those whose desire leads them to seek the Tao and are ready to seek their Master.

And the pupil sat.

TATOO COUPON

25

TATOO COUPON

The Tao Of Silence

And the pupil asked:

My Master, how shall I learn to do only good, so that my life may have some meaning?

The Master replied:

Who knows what is good? Even God reveals the good in man in numerous ways! And every good differs from another. Therefore when a deed is done, only the doer knows if it good or bad.

And the pupil stared.

The Tao Of Silence

If you posses nothing, if you belong to nothing, you have made the first step in the Tao of Silence. Now all that you must learn is to tell good from bad.

The Tao Of Silence

An easy life is not an ally to the Tao of Silence. Senseless pride is the enemy of the Tao.

The Tao Of Silence

When I came to study the Tao,
I built a stone hut in the desert,

and from that day on I ate only bread,
brought to me by the sweat of my brow,

and from that day on I spoke only words,
which I would not regret even
on my dying day.

And still I seek the Tao of Silence.

The Tao Of Silence

And the pupil asked:

Why, my Master, do you reject so many who come to learn the Tao of Silence?

The Master replied:

He who comes not in humility, it is best to turn away; he who judges another, it is best to turn away.

And the pupil bowed his head.

The Tao Of Silence

And the pupil asked:

Why, my Master, are the pupils served full bowls and bread spiced with salt, oil, and vinegar, while the teachers are served half-filled bowls?

The Master replied:

Only he who has everything laid before him may choose a little. He who has studied the Tao of Silence will restrain his stomach even at a banquet of kings. He who has no food before him — how should he restrain his stomach?

And the pupil ate.

The Tao Of Silence

He who chooses the Tao of Silence —
hates evil.

He who chooses the Tao of Silence —
will not join the evildoer.

He who chooses the Tao of Silence —
will not seek the place of evil.

He who chooses the Tao of Silence —
will tend to his own business.

He who chooses the Tao of Silence —
will give and not take.

He who chooses the Tao of Silence —
will not hold senseless jealousy in his heart.

He who chooses the Tao of Silence —
will not be a glutton.

The Tao Of Silence

He who does all this —
The Tao of Silence will reside in his heart.

The Tao Of Silence

The pupil asked:

I have learned, my Master, that I must guard my tongue and restrain my stomach, beware of foolish pride and not lose my senses to wine or drugs. What more have I to learn?

The Master replied:

Learn not to argue with anyone even though you may disagree with him. When he speaks the truth, say "Yes;" when he lies say: "Surely you know what you are saying!" But never argue about something already said. Thus, only, will your soul listen and hear the Tao of Silence.

And the pupil heard.

The Tao Of Silence

The desert is the place of Tao, where man can better hear silence than amongst the city tumult. A fish, cast on land, will die without water around him. Tao will disappear without silence. Silence will disappear without Tao. If we return the fish to water we return him to his life. If we return the silence to Tao we return to the right path.

The Tao Of Silence

The Tao Master asked the Supreme Master, the Enlightener:

"How am I to contain the Tao of Silence in my life?"

"Go to the desert, and sit there with yourself, in solitude," answered the Enlightener.

Years later, the Enlightener passed the hut of the Tao Master, who came outside to greet him.

"Thank you, Enlightener, for showing me the Tao of Silence," he said.

But the Enlightener only scowled and said:

"Indeed, you have preserved the Tao of Silence in your life, instead of living the Tao of Silence day in day out, hour after hour. Is this the way to the Tao of Silence?"

And the Master bowed his head, acknowledging his mistake. For he who lives among the crowd, according to the

The Tao Of Silence

rules of the Tao of Silence, is worthy of being a Tao Master; he who sits in the desert, will only be a Master to the rocks about him.

And he took up his stick immediately and departed for the city.

The Tao Of Silence

A pupil of the Tao went to his Master and asked him to provide him with one word through which he may find the Tao. The Master sent him to the silence, for there in the solitude of silence may the pupil find the Tao.

The Tao Of Silence

A Tao pupil burst into great laughter during the morning meditation. Another pupil rebuked him:

"How dare you laugh while we seek the silence?"

The instructor, who guides the pupils of the Tao, intervened:

"Who is to say where the silence lies? In laughter or in crying, in solitude or in a crowd?"

And the Master said:

"And perhaps he who looks inside his soul and laughter fills him, has already found the silence?"

The Tao Of Silence

The Tao Master known as "the Stone Carrier" carried a stone in his mouth, day and night for seven years, until he found the Tao of Silence. He was the first in the silent monastery who denied his tongue of words.

Do we learn from this that the Tao of Silence is to be found in the silent stone?

The Tao Of Silence

What is the book called, "The Tao of Silence?"

In the desert, many years ago, lived a Tao Master who set off each morning to the hills, sat on a rock, and read a book.

One of his pupils saw him and coveted the book, thinking it was valuable. One night he entered the Master's room, took the book, and slipped away to the next town.

In the town the pupil sought a book dealer and offered him the book for the price of one hundred gold coins. The book dealer wondered at the price and asked the pupil to leave him the book, that he may find out its worth. And so it happened.

The book dealer went to the Tao Master, who was a known authority on books, and asked him if the book was worth one hundred gold coins. The Master examined the book and replied, "Indeed, this book is very valuable."

The book dealer returned to town and paid the pupil one hundred gold coins, and

The Tao Of Silence

afterwards told him that he had been to see the Master, who told him of the value of the book.

"And what else did he tell you?" asked the pupil, in fear.

"Nothing. He speaks little," answered the book dealer.

The pupil's conscience was disturbed and he returned the gold to the man and went to the Master. There he knelt and asked forgiveness, returning the book to the Master.

And from that day on the pupil lived with the Master and was faithful to him in all his heart and soul. And the two of them departed each morning to the hills to read the book.

It was the book called "The Tao of Silence," but it could be any other book that leads the pupil to his destined Master.

The Tao Of Silence

Why are the spirits of the day and the spirits of the night afraid of the path of silence?

Because he who learns to control his tongue will never speak evil of another and, therefore, the spirits will have no hold upon his life. The Tao of Silence is the complete opposite of the path of all spirits.

The Tao Of Silence

And the pupil asked:

Many times, in order to correct another's ways, anger arises in my heart. Will the amendment atone for the arising anger?

The Master replied:

He who loses himself in order to save another, loses the Tao of silence.

The pupil nodded.

The Tao Of Silence

It is better to fill the stomach with meat and wine than to fill the heart with jealousy and resentment for another.

The Tao Of Silence

One day a pupil of the Tao found a bottle of wine in a cellar and, forgetting himself, he sipped it all and became intoxicated. His fellow pupils found him wallowing in his vomit and rebuked him.

"Do not rebuke him," their Master stopped them. "If he had not sipped the whole bottle we would all be taking sips. Thank him for withholding the wine from you and do not rebuke him."

The Tao Of Silence

A Tao pupil was walking down a path. Alongside him walked three young girls, chatting loudly, distracting the pupil from his contemplation. When he returned to his Master he reported what had happened: "...and it was the blue-eyed one who spoke loudly to the one with red ribbons in her hair, whilst the third, light-haired..."

Here the Master stopped him:

"If you had been meditating on the Tao of Silence while walking, you would not have noticed if it were man or woman walking beside you on the path. And what is the sound of girlish chatter compared to the din of your anxious soul!"

The Tao Of Silence

Burdened with many packages, a pupil of the Tao of Silence came to his Master. When the Master saw his circumstances he gave him a gold coin and instructed him to go to town, purchase a large piece of meat, and return, carrying it on his back.

The pupil followed the instructions; on his return, the smell of the meat attracted birds of prey and stray dogs, who pecked and nipped at his legs.

He returned to his Master without the meat, his body wounded and bitten.

"Here," said the Master, "he who enslaves himself to possessions attracts the spirits of the day and the spirits of the night, such as birds of prey and stray dogs, and is destined to carry the scars on his back his entire life."

The Tao Of Silence

When one has a book, a picture, or an object which fills his life with light, this is good.

When one has a book, a picture, or an object which fills his life with darkness, this is bad.

How may the good become bad?

How may the bad become good?

He who knows the Tao of Silence will know.

The Tao Of Silence

I know a man who for seventy years studied all that one can study, and still he did not know the Tao of Silence.

The Tao Of Silence

Desire and silence, never shall they walk the same path.

The Tao Of Silence

How may I reach the end of the path?

In order to reach the beginning of the path, you must know the goal and bear patiently the burden of the path, in the right spirit. When you do this you will know the end of the path.

The Tao Of Silence

A tree, if we prune it day after day, will never bear fruit.

So too is the man who learns the Tao of Silence. If he changes his opinion every day, he will never acquire any knowledge.

The Tao Of Silence

Solitude is like the revelation of the almighty to humankind,
> bringing enlightenment to his spirit;

solitude resembles the existence of the dark grave,
> leading man for his destruction.

The Tao of Silence choose between enlightenment and destruction.

The Tao Of Silence

A well-known philosopher who wrote tens of books came to study the Tao of Silence. He sat opposite the Tao Master and begged him, again and again, to convey the principles of the Tao. But the Master sat before him and did not speak a word. One day passed, another day passed, and on the third day the philosopher despaired and left.

One of the Master's pupils wondered at this and questioned the Master about his strange behavior.

"All he desired was to learn the Tao of Silence," said the pupil.

"He did not seek the Tao," replied the Master. "He is a merchant of words who seeks merchandise in the verse of strangers in order to market them himself."

The Tao Of Silence

And the pupil asked:

Why Master should I learn the Tao of Silence? For I have never experienced it.

The Master replied:

Never have you tarred a road, never have you built a ship, never have you raised a bridge — still you travel the road, you sail the ship, and you cross bridge. The Tao of Silence will teach you the nature of things so you will be able to experience them in spirit, without actually doing them, for the essence of things, all things, will be in your heart.

And the pupil nodded.

The Tao Of Science

When a person tells you he is a fool, believe him.

The Tao Of Silence

When the life of glamour and arrogance replaces the peaceful soul, temptations become the refuge of man.

The Tao Of Silence

And the pupil asked:

Why, my Master, do I see you working every morning in your garden, in order to eat the food that you have planted with your very hands.

Is it not worthy of a man of the spirit to dedicate all his time to study and contemplation?

The Master arose, removed some books from one of the shelves, handed them to the pupil, and said: "Go, dear pupil, read, study, and memorize these books in order to contemplate the teachings."

The pupil retired to his room and began to read, to study, and to memorize. One hour passed, two hours, the entire day, and still no one called him for dinner. Finally, overcome with hunger, he found his Master and complained, "Master, shall we eat nothing today? Surely today is not a day of fasting."

The Tao Of Silence

The Master replied, "We have eaten our portion of bread today. But you prefer study and contemplation to food, so I assumed you would not be hungry."

The pupil's face was vexed, having been shown his mistake, and he returned the books to their shelf, promising his Master never to underestimate labor of the hands.

And the pupil ate.

The Tao Of Silence

A teacher sold his book, from which he taught the Tao of Silence, and gave the money to a needy person who was begging beside his house. It was said of this teacher, "he knew not what he taught," for he gave a gift to a beggar instead of giving the money to a needy man who works for his living. For without work there is no Tao, and without Tao there is no silence.

The Tao Of Silence

A pupil saw a fellow pupil jokingly provoking a girl in the street and immediately went to the Master to inform him of the incident, in hope that the pupil would be reprimanded and his status undermined. The Master heard him and summoned the pupil, speaking with him for over one hour and requesting that he describe the girl's beautiful figure, over and over again.

The Tao Of Silence

A teacher of the Tao announced that he would allow only male pupils in his court, never female ones, for woman by her nature cannot learn the Tao.

And the Master of the Tao of Silence heard this and brought a gift to the new teacher — a sack, which according to him was filled with firewood. The teacher-of-no-female-pupils took the sack and saw that it was filled with ash, incapable of nourishing a fire. He gazed in awe at the Master of the Tao of Silence, asked him the meaning of this.

"You are of woman born, yet you claim to be better than woman. Could the smoke of the fire be of higher quality than the burning fire? Please teach me how the ash may take the place of firewood?"

And the teacher bowed his head in shame and on that day dissolved his court and returned to study the Tao of Silence, this time with the Mistress of the Tao of Silence, she who was called "Silent Tao Mother."

The Tao Of Silence

A group of pupils walking along a path were suddenly attacked by a group of bandits.

The pupils shouted and cried for help and, luckily, a few policemen appeared, apprehended the bandits, and escorted them to prison.

The Tao pupils continued walking along the path, talking amongst themselves. One of them boasted of his bravery in the face of the bandits, another offered an amazing rendition of his screams, and yet another displayed his wounds with pride.

Finally one of the pupils, who had up until then been silent, spoke:

"I do not know, friends, if we behaved as one should. Surely because of us people are now sitting in prison. I wonder if we should not have offered our possessions to the bandits in order to prevent this course of events which has ended with people of flesh and blood behind bars."

The Tao Of Silence

His words were so persuasive that regret hung over the group of pupils. In consensus, they hurried to the house of the Master of the Tao of Silence to request his advice.

The Master greeted them, heard their story, and bowed his head without speaking a word.

The pupils waited one hour, two hours, three hours, until finally one of them dared to ask the Master to answer the question they had posed.

And the Master answered:

He who readily gives his possessions over to bandits will indeed strengthen the greed in their hearts - and will do wrong; and he who brings the bandits to imprisonment, betrays humankind - and will do wrong. Therefore, perhaps it is not your fault, and not the fault of the bandits, but simply the fault of possessions. For in our desire to obtain them, and in our desire

The Tao Of Silence

to preserve them, we commit the gravest of all sins.

The pupils departed on their way and after a short time they again began arguing, one saying that the Master had justified their actions, another saying that he had justified the bandits.

The Tao Of Silence

And the pupil asked:

Master, please guide me in my actions. Everyday when I come to your courtyard, the people on the wayside abuse me, throwing stones and setting their dogs on me. My Master, may I return a blow for their blows?

His fellow pupils hastened to shake their heads, "No, no."

The Master replied:

Carry a heavy staff and cast your blows on them that they may learn proper behavior. For he who lets this behavior go by, day after day, will teach the people that this is the way of the world. And after you have beaten them, if your pain is greater than theirs, then you will know that you beat them in the way of the Tao of Silence.

And the pupil was amazed.

The Tao Of Silence

A pupil of the Tao of Silence, whose name was then Pen Lo, was as ugly as a monkey; wherever he went, people mocked him and insulted him because of his appearance. The pupil came to the Master and requested his help.

The Master said: "Gather all your money, my pupil, and take to the road. And during the course of an entire year, offer one silver coin to every person who mocks or insults you."

The pupil wondered at this, but, being faithful, accepted the advice of his Master. He collected all his money, put it in his backpack, and departed. And every time he was mocked or insulted, smiling in surrender he took a silver coin from his backpack and handed it to the perpetrator. At the end of the year, his money ran out and so he returned to the Master and asked him what to do.

"Nothing," replied the Master, "Go on your way."

The pupil went. An impudent merchant saw him and mocked his appearance. The pupil heard him and burst into laughter.

The Tao Of Silence

"Thank you, my friend," he shouted to the merchant. "Until now I have paid a silver coin for such blessings, and you grant me your blessing free of charge! Thank you!"

And from that day the pupil was, in his own eyes, the same as any other man in figure and appearance.

The Tao Of Silence

A certain pupil used to obey the rules of the Tao with extreme devotion, especially with relation to food. Every time bread and vegetables were served to his table, he partook only from the bread; every time meat was served, he adamantly refused it; and never would he take a second helping.

"For me," he would proclaim, "water, salt, and bread, is enough for sustenance."

He behaved in this manner for one month, at the close of which the Master of the Tao of Silence summoned him to his quarters and instructed him to eat his food in the solitude of his room and not with the other pupils.

"Why, honorable Master?" exclaimed the pupil. "Certainly I attempt to set an example for the others..."

"It is not your stomach that you must overcome," said the Master, "but your name as one who abstains from everything.

> The Tao Of Silence

You cause those around you to seem gluttonous and self-satisfying, and full of lust for eating. You forget that humility is the first merit in the Tao of Silence!"

And from that day forward the pupil cared with more discipline for his humility than his stomach.

The Tao Of Silence

The Tao pupil who lived in a sinful town moved to another town in order to avoid the evil. Immediately three sinners moved into his house!

The Master of the Tao of Silence heard this and sent the pupil directly to his former home. Not having a house in which to live, the three sinners quit the town.

The Tao Of Silence

A wealthy man went to a philosopher for advice: "Tell me, wisest of men, where may I find happiness?"

The philosopher contemplated a long while and finally sent the man to a large library, to find his happiness in books.

The man went to a great master and repeated his question. The latter sent him to a solitary monastery.

The man went to a religious teacher who sent him the great temple.

Thus the man went from master to master, from wise man to wise man. This one sent him to seek solitude among hilltops, that one sent him to please himself in a house of pleasure, this one promised him life in the next world, and that one sent him to work in this world.

And although the man was a faithful and devoted pupil, accepting the advice of his teachers, he did not find happiness.

The Tao Of Silence

Finally he reached the Master of the Tao of Silence and, his voice weary, he repeated his question: "Where am I to find happiness, Master of the Tao of Silence?"

The Master of the Tao of Silence contemplated a long while and then answered briefly:

"In the place that you lost your happiness, that is where you will find your happiness."

The Tao Of Silence

A pupil of the Tao of Silence, who studied in the company of other pupils, sinned. The pupils gathered and decided to expel the sinner from their small group. The went to tell the Master of the Tao of Silence of the incident.

"You have done well," the Master of the Tao of Silence praised the pupils, "and in order to strengthen your hearts I will leave with the sinner, so I may rid my heart of sin and leave you unstained."

And so the Master and the pupil who sinned departed, leaving behind the group of pupils, silent and astounded.

The Tao Of Silence

A prince who lived in a large city accused his son of a great sin and sought to bring him to justice. But none of the judges in the city were prepared to judge the son. The prince sent for the Master of the Tao of Silence who lived outside the city walls, to judge the son.

The Master of the Tao of Silence arrived at the palace with a heavy chain, like that in which prisoners are bound, wrapped around his waist and dragging noisily behind him.

"Why do you drag this chain with you?" asked the prince.

"Can you not see, my prince! It is my sins that I have bound around my waist, and I drag them wherever I go, so that all may see evil and choose good," answered the Master of the Tao of Silence.

The prince looked upon the Master, bound to a chain attached to nothing, and then sent him on his way. And how can a master, who does not see his own sins, judge the sins of others.

The Tao Of Silence

And the pupil asked:

I sit in my cell, contemplate the Tao of Silence, meditate, and still I am unable to find peace and my soul is agitated. Is it the solitude of my cell that does this to me?

And the Master replied:

When a pupil brings the treasures of his past into the solitude of the Tao, shadows fill his soul and tranquillity will not abide, even in his solitude. Only when the pupil brings the tranquillity of his past, will the latter fill his spirit and his soul and pave the way for the Tao of Silence.

The Tao Of Silence

The pupil asked again:

I do not understand what you have said Master.

The Master replied:

Now you are on the right track.

And the pupil was silent.

The Tao Of Silence

Only the sinner can judge the sinner;

Only the sinner can judge the straight-pathed;

And who will judge the straight-pathed judge?

The Tao Of Silence

The Master of the Tao of Silence saw his gifted pupil eating in a vulgar manner in the tavern, clowning amongst jokers and mocking his friends.

When the pupil noticed his Master he hastened to him and hung his head in shame:

"Forgive me, honorable Master! I promise to fast for a week, atone for my sins with great devotion, and sleep on the bare ground..."

The Master nodded and said quietly:

"Good, but first finish your dinner, drink your glass of liquor, and finish what you were saying."

This said, he departed.

The Tao Of Silence

A pupil sought to learn the Tao of Silence in a solitary monastery lead by a group of religious teachers. Upon his arrival he promised them to do all he could in order to be as one of the angels, the servants of God, and never to degrade himself with mortal behavior, mortal lust, or mortal needs.

"And who will prepare your meals? And who will clean your room? And who will draw water from the well for you?" one of the teachers asked him.

"He whose angel I will be," answered the pupil. "God will supply me my needs."

The teacher took his hand and brought him to the old farmer who managed the household affairs of the monastery.

"Meet the God whose angel you are," said the teacher.

The Tao Of Silence

And the pupil asked:

Whose conduct is better, Master of the Tao of Silence - he who locks up his thoughts and reflections or he who expresses them and discusses them in public?

The Master replied:

He who keeps his clothes in a sealed chest, and does not air them out for a long time, and does not wear them, will later find his clothes damp and moldy. Did he do well by keeping his clothes in a sealed chest?

The pupil continued to ask:

Surely he who wears his clothes is bound to soil them and tear them. Is it not better to keep his clothes in a chest?

The Master replied:

The nature of a piece of clothing is to be worn. The nature of a thought is to become knowledge. The nature of a reflection is to become words. And he who does not fulfill his nature, is he preferable to one who fulfills his nature, even at the price of a tear or a stain?

And the pupil understood.

The Tao Of Science

Five pupils of the Tao came to eat at the Master's table. The Master laid ten trays of food before them. The pupils wondered who would be joining them for dinner.

"Speak," the Master told them. "And soon you will discover that ten opinions sit at the table!"

The Tao Of Silence

A certain teacher taught his pupils to return a good deed for a bad one, to love he that hates you, and to always return a soft word for a hard one. The pupils of the Tao of Silence came to their Master and asked, "Should we not do best to take the path of this teacher? Surely his path will make us among the sublime of all men?"

"You are well and fortunate," replied the Master of the Tao of Silence. "Oh that I should be worthy to be part of a group so sublime in thought."

The Tao Of Silence

A pupil approached the Master of the Tao of Silence and said to him:

"My thoughts are disturbed, Master. I try to capture my thoughts and they escape me. What am I to do?"

"Go and catch the wind in flight," said the Master of the Tao of Silence.

The pupil stared at him in amazement:

"How shall I catch the wind in flight? Surely the wind is faster than any man."

"You are unable to catch the slow wind, yet you try to catch your thoughts whose speed has no match?" wondered the Master.

The Tao Of Silence

There is a man who has carried an ax for his entire life and has never chopped down a tree.

Is it an ax that he carries or simply a tool for which he has no use?

The Tao Of Silence

A Master of the Tao of Silence must teach faithfully what he knows.

A pupil of the Tao of Silence must study faithfully what he does not know.

Therefore a Master of the Tao of Silence must teach faithfully what the pupil does not know.

Therefore the pupil of the Tao must study faithfully what the Master does not know.

And who is the teacher? And who is the pupil?

The Tao Of Silence

One who plants his roots in a certain place but does not give fruit to the place, the place will cast him out from his roots. For it is not the roots which hold one in his place but the fruit which he offers to the place.

The Tao Of Science

And the pupil asked:

Is it best for me, Master, to walk the straight path? Or would it be better for me to choose the crooked path on which my spirit leads me?

The Master replied:

He who takes the straight path north, sees the north.
He who takes the straight path south, sees the south.
He who takes the straight path east, sees the east.
He who takes the straight path west, sees the west
And he who walks the crooked path, sees all the directions.

And the pupil saw.

The Tao Of Science

There is no harm in a bad thought.

The harm lies in the realization of the bad thought.

The Tao Of Silence

And the pupil asked:

Master, which pupil do you prefer - the one who eats more than he needs to and whose hunger is not satisfied, or the one who eats less than his needs and is satisfied?

The Master replied:

He who is not satisfied overcomes his hunger. And he who is satisfied, what does he overcome?

The Tao Of Silence

He who lends an ear to gossip and satanic speech is like a house fortified against bandits whose gate is locked, whose lock is secure, and whose windows are wide open.

The Tao Of Silence

A man came to the Master of the Tao of Silence, complaining, "Sorrow and grief fill my days and nights!"

"He who leaves his days empty and his nights desolate, should not be surprised to find an uninvited visitor in the empty space," replied the Master.

The Tao Of Silence

A teacher, well-known throughout the land, possessed the power to curse anyone who angered him. His name became so glorified that he was known to all as "The Greatest Master of All."

And who throughout the entire country knew the Master who had the power to bless.

The Tao Of Silence

When the pupils of the Tao of Silence began to study, throughout the day they discussed the good in man and the exhaltation of the soul and the correct path which leads to enlightenment. And when they were familiar with their studies they began to discuss all the evil in the world, the evil gossip and destructive ignorance. And of this the Master of the Tao of Silence said, "Better to be an innocent ignoramus, than a proud student."

› The Tao Of Silence ‹

On the door of the Master of the Tao of Silence's quarters someone carved, in thick letters:

**When you see a pupil trying to reach
the highest enlightenment,
quickly hold his belt,
so that his feet do not lose their
connection with the ground.**

The Tao Of Silence

A pupil who hears with his eyes and sees with his ears will not forget what he learns.

The Tao Of Silence

Accept the Tao of Silence,

Do not think idle thoughts,

Contemplate quietly when you are alone, as well as when you are in public, as well as when you study, and as well as when you work,

And evil will find no place in your heart.

The Tao Of Silence

One morning the Master of the Tao of Silence arose from his seat and led his pupils into the field. There they saw an ox tethered to a beam, his eyes covered, pacing round and round, pulling the beam, drawing water from the well.

"Look at the ox," said the Master. "When his eyes are covered his course is set by man. So too is the man whose eyes are covered and who does not see what is in front of him — evil thought takes hold of him and leads him wherever it desires."

The Tao Of Silence

A group of merchants returned from the market and passed the house of the Master of the Tao of Silence. One of the merchants suggested they stop at the Master's house to pay their respects.

The merchants turned to the Master's house and he received them warmly with food and drink, after which he sent them on with a blessing. His pupils wondered at his behavior, for merchants are full of greed and the Master's time is precious, dedicated entirely to study and contemplation. Why then did he find it fitting to receive the merchants?

"It was not the merchants who met my eyes," answered the Master. "But the women and children, the workers and laborers, who the merchants support and nourish. Am I, one who works for spirit and soul, worthier than the man who works for himself and others?"

The Tao Of Silence

A pupil of the Tao went to the east and there he studied the theory of the one-hundred. He returned to the Master of the Tao of Silence and asked him:

"Master, if ninety-nine people tell me that I am a fish, I am still human. But if a hundredth person tells me that I am a fish — would I not then be a fish?"

"How powerful the hundredth person is, that he can, by an idle word, transform human into fish," said the Master of the Tao of Silence. "Now gather one hundred wise men, go to the stream, and turn the fish to human by the power of the theory of one-hundred."

[The Theory of One Hundred defines the united power of quantity as quality. If one monkey speaks human language — this is still chance. But if the hundredth monkey speaks human language, perhaps the conclusion is that human language is the language of apes, and it is but chance that the rest of the monkeys are not familiar with this language.]

The Tao Of Silence

One of the Masters of the Tao of Silence became a hermit, turned to the desert, and settled in a far corner, where no man had ever laid his feet. Seven years passed, and to this meager tent came a wanderer on his way through the desert. When he saw the Master, he quickly packed his belongings and prepared to continue on his way.

"I will not disturb you, Honorable Master," said the wanderer. "I am only passing and will immediately carry on so as not to disturb your solitude."

"Wherever you are going I shall go with you," said the Tao Master. "The solitude which I have accumulated inside me is so great that even amongst a crowd of people I will not be able to disconnect from it."

Later the three departed - the wanderer, the Master, and the solitude - leaving the desert behind.

The Tao Of Silence

One of the teachers of the Tao of Silence who was formerly married and with a family, fled to the desert and made his home in a place in which no woman had ever been seen. Years passed and the teacher aged, and knowing that his end was drawing near, he decided to return to a place of human settlement.

One of his pupils wondered: "Master, surely there are many women there? And all your life you have kept your distance from the company of women."

"On the contrary," replied the teacher. "The more years that have passed, the clearer were the women in my dreams, until they touched my soul, becoming still clearer."

And after all those years he made his way to the house that had been his home and to the family which was his own to ask forgiveness for his flight into the desert.

The Tao Of Silence

A Master of the Tao of Silence went to his Master, sat at his feet, and asked:

"Master please advise me. I have learned to find the silence in the water element. I have learned to find the silence in the earth element. I have learned to find the silence in the element of air. What am I to learn now?"

His Master raised his hand and spread his fingers. The sun shone through his fingers so that they seemed to have caught fire.

"This is what I have wanted to learn all my life," said the Master of the Master. "How to find the silence in fire. Learn this, and then return to teach me this Tao."

The Tao Of Silence

The pupils sat in a crowded row at the dinner table when suddenly one of them spilt his cup, soiling his shirt.

Immediately the Master of the Tao of Silence raised his cup, pouring its contents on his shirt.

The Tao Of Silence

"Why in order to learn my soul, must I study the Tao of Silence?" asked the pupil.

The Master led him to the courtyard, to the small pool of water, and directed him to gaze in its waters. The pupil saw the reflection of his portrait and wondered what his Master wanted to teach him.

The Master took a stick and stirred the water, the sharp portrait blurring and becoming incomprehensible.

"Just as you cannot see your portrait in the stormy water, thus you cannot see your soul when you are troubled inside and your awareness storms like rough waters," said the Master of the Tao of Silence.

The Tao Of Silence

The Master of the Tao of Silence went to visit a friend and celebrate with him. Upon arriving at his friend's house, he behaved there as any one of the guests - eating in a vulgar manner, sipping too much wine, and speaking loudly and idly. When the party ended, his friend accompanied him on his way, apologizing:

"I am sorry that I caused you to eat so, to become intoxicated, and to waste your time in idle chatter."

"Did I do all that?" wondered the Master of the Tao of Silence. "It seems to me that it was the visitor in your house who did all those deeds and not me!"

The Tao Of Silence

A group of Tao pupils, who lived near a noisy town, despaired at attempting to positively influence the inhabitants. It seemed that their labor was pointless, the people not displaying the least improvement. The pupils turned to the Master of the Tao of Silence and asked his advice.

"In my youth," the Master told them, "I saw two farmers who worked identical plots of land. The soil was hard, and the well was dry. One of the farmers worked the land with the sweat of his brow, planting and sowing his harvest, even though it was so meager he did not even manage to collect one sack of wheat. The other farmer saw the situation and did not bother to work his field at all. The next year there was famine and shortage, and I remember that one loaf of bread was worth its weight in gold. And who was it that survived, he and all his household? He who behaved as a man of wisdom and forsook his field, or he who behaved as a man of belief and worked his field?"

The Tao Of Silence

Obedience is human nature.

The slave obeys others.

The free man obeys himself.

The Tao Of Silence

One day the Master of the Tao of Silence took up an ancient book, written by a philosopher who was known throughout five continents and seven oceans, and read a portion of his book to his pupils. He then asked the meaning of the portion.

The pupils were happy to display their familiarity with the book and one after the other provided wonderful interpretations of the portion they had heard, one relating it to the secret of creation, another connecting it with the secret of tranquillity. Finally, the Master turned to one of the pupils, a modest and quiet son of a farmer.

"And you, can you interpret the section? Do you know what message it conveys?" he asked.

"I do not know," replied the pupil with humility.

"He who does not know is the one who will find the way to the Tao of Silence," said the Master, quietly.

The Tao Of Silence

Humility and modesty are the rungs of the ladder which raise self-awareness to the highest enlightenment.

The Tao Of Silence

A teacher of the Tao of Silence, known as "the one who sits on the highest step," met Satan once while on his way to the mountain. Satan detained him, complaining:

"Tell me, teacher of the Tao, why do I not succeed in going your way, and reaching enlightenment and awareness? When you fast one day, I fast seven days! When you contemplate one night, I contemplate seven nights! When you give a coin for charity I give a handful of coins! And still I am Satan, and you are the Supreme Master. Why?"

And the teacher of the Tao of Silence raised his eyes to the heavens and thanked the Creator of all for not granting Satan modesty and humility.

The Tao Of Silence

The Master of the Tao of Silence said to his pupils:

Never behave in your home as if you were a visitor,

Never let name and fame pave the way before you,

Never wonder about what you will be after death,

Always be at peace with all people.

These are the four worldly rules that every person seeks, in life and in death.

The Tao Of Science

Inhaling, man takes in the essence of the universe.

Exhaling, man offers his essence to the universe.

Is this not the process of creation?

The Tao Of Silence

The Tao pupil asked the Master:

"When, Master, will I know I have learned the Tao of Silence?

The Tao Master answered the pupil:

When you forgive the one who hurts you, even before he requests your forgiveness, before even the thought of remorse has risen within him - know that you have learned the Tao of Silence.

The Tao Of Silence

A Tao teacher taught his pupils to return a good deed to those who wrong them, this being the test of the Tao for them.

The Master of the Tao of Silence rebuked him:

If we return good deeds for bad deeds, surely we will encourage the bad and cause another to continue doing wrong for the purification of our soul. This is not the way. When we encounter someone who means bad, we will do well to look down and walk away from him, keeping silent. This is the way of the Tao of Silence.

The Tao Of Science

A governor of a certain country felt that his life was unfulfilled and that his soul was empty, and so he went to find peace of mind. He wandered many paths, climbed hilltops, visited monasteries and temples, consulted the wise men of various countries, and still he could not find peace of mind. Seven years later he returned to his country. Upon approaching his palace, a girl and a boy hurried to him, "Father, where have you been?" cried the children, who had been merely infants when he set out on his journey.

And suddenly there was peace in his heart.

The Tao Of Silence

Silence is like drops of rain.

Silence is like grains of sand -

If silence has no limits,

it will swallow up the entire world.

The Tao Of Silence

One day the Master of the Tao of Silence led his pupils up to the bare peak of a mountain.

The rain did not cease to pour, the wind pounded the rocky slopes, but the Master did not stop until they had ascended the peak. When they arrived, he instructed the pupils to light a fire.

The pupils scattered about the bare slopes to gather twigs and branches. They piled the wood and, for a long hour, attempted to light a fire. Smoke blinded their eyes, and time and time again the wind and rain put out the embers. Only after a great effort was the fire lit, glowing warm and bright.

And when the fire burned, the Tao Master turned and descended from the mountain, his pupils after him. A long time after their descent, the fire continued to burn.

The Tao Of Silence

This is the way of the Tao of Silence, with great effort we will light the fire of silence, despite the rain, the wind, and the smoke.

And at the end of the path we will find the fire, bright and warming.

The Tao Of Silence

In ancient Egypt there lived a famous monk, known the world over for the life of celibacy he took upon himself. He drank rainwater and licked dew off the rocks, and his only food was millet and barley. His clothing consisted of a simple sack, and he slept on the bare earth of a small stone cave.

A group of idle passers-by heard of his fame and decided, as a prank, to test him. They hired a famous prostitute, familiar with all seven temptations, paid her a fair amount of money and sent her to the monk, promising that if she managed to seduce him she would receive a large reward.

That night the prostitute arrived at the entrance of the cave and in a tearful voice cried, "Help! Help!"

The monk heard her cry and, emerging from his cave, saw the distressed woman. She told him that bandits had attacked her and stole the wagon she was riding. The monk suggested she sit at the entrance of his cave until morning, when

The Tao Of Silence

he would lead her to town and she would be able to carry on her way.

The monk returned to the cave, but the prostitute continued sobbing, saying that she was afraid of wild animals. The monk took her inside the cave, and at her request he lit a fire in the hearth. And she, who had men falling at her feet, tried to seduce him in every way she knew.

The monk, whose flesh cried out with lust, quickly put his finger in the fire so that the pain would stop the passions of his heart.

And she continued.

And during the night, the monk singed his fingers one by one, until his flesh blackened.

In the morning, the idle passers-by hurried to the cave, and knowing that the monk could tell no lie, they asked him what the woman had done to him during the night. And he held up his burnt hands and said: "Nothing. Everything that I did, I did to myself in order not to yield to her seductions."

The Tao Of Science

Upon seeing what she had done, the woman immediately suffered a stroke, fell to the ground, and did not arise.

The monk, who became known from that day as "the black-fingered one," prayed to his gods, and returned to his celibacy.

The Tao Of Silence

When the Master of the Tao of Silence heard the story, he contemplated a long while and then asked the storyteller:

"Indeed, the monk overcame his lust. But did he also overcome the sin of pride? So proud was he in his celibacy, that he was prepared to sacrifice his flesh for it, as well as the spirit of the woman. Would it not have been better to give in to temptation and to ask forgiveness?"

The Tao Of Silence

One night, bandits entered the house of the Tao Master, bound him to a chair, and emptied the house of all its valuables. Later, they released the Master and carried on their way.

After a short while, the Tao Master realized that the bandits had not noticed the box in which he stored his money. He immediately took up the box and hurried after the thieves, shouting, "Wait one moment! Wait! You forgot to steal my money!"

The bandits, seeing what a righteous man he was, were shamed. They returned his belongings to the Master and reverted from their bad ways.

And the Master of the Tao of Silence said, "What power has the iron lock, that it can chase bandits from the house of a righteous man!"

The Tao Of Silence

One night, bandits entered the house of the Tao Master, bound him to a chair, and emptied the house of all its valuables. Later, they released the Master and carried on their way.

After a short while, the Tao Master realized that the bandits had not noticed the box in which he stored his money. He immediately took up the box and hurried after the thieves, shouting, "Wait one moment! Wait! You forgot to steal my money!"

The bandits, seeing what a fool he was, mocked him, beat his head, and continued on their way, leaving him beaten and injured, on the side of the road.

And the Master of the Tao of Silence said, "What power has the iron lock, that it can chase bandits from the house of a fool!"

The Tao Of Silence

There are those who seek refuge from worldly illness, illusions, and evils, in the Tao of Silence.

The Tao Of Silence

And there are those, more sublime, who seek in the Tao of Silence the source of strength to fight all worldly illness, illusions, and evils.

The Tao Of Silence

A monk decided that he would stand on one leg atop the mountain and fast for seventy days and seventy nights, forgoing sleep and rest. Masses of believers gathered to see the human wonder.

One day passed, two days passed, three days passed, at the end of nine days, the monk collapsed as rye at the hands of the harvester. And the masses of believers cursed and mocked him for having failed in the task which he had undertaken.

And only the pupil of the Tao of Silence who was present, approached the monk, treated him, took him to his cabin, and fed him as he recovered. And no one came to cheer the pupil and to witness the human wonder.

The Tao Of Science

And the pupil asked:

Master, there is a man who owes me a small amount of money. Am I to go to him and request my money?

The Master replied:

Go and ask for your money, humbly and in low spirits.

The Tao Of Silence

A while later the pupil returned and asked:

Master, there is a man who owes me a small amount of money. I asked him for it but I did not receive it. Am I to go and ask again?

The Master replied:

Collect the amount that the man owes you and give it to him as charity. Learn to hear the wordless request.

And the pupil was embarrassed.

The Tao Of Silence

The Master of the Tao of Silence took his pupils to see the work of the honey seeker. The latter found a beehive in an old tree trunk, chased away the bees with smoke, chopped down the tree with an ax, and removed the honey.

"The tree is like a man," said the Master of the Tao of Silence. "Life is like smoke; death is like the ax. The honey is the inner enlightenment. Do not let life or death bring out the enlightenment - look for it in the person himself."

The Tao Of Silence

A man came to the Master of the Tao of Silence and asked him:

How can I become a pupil of the Tao of Silence?

And the Master of the Tao of Silence replied:

Stay.

The Tao Of Silence

It is better to labor lightly over a long period,

Than to labor arduously for a short time.

And that is the Tao of Silence.

The Tao Of Science

Beware not to take the thoughts of others into the thoughts of your sleep.

The Tao Of Silence

A pupil who does not overcome his rage at
the time of anger,

will not overcome his lust at
the time of passion,

will not overcome his gluttony at
the time of hunger.

He is not a pupil of the Tao of Silence.

The Tao Of Silence

Keep away from any man who has "no" on his tongue more than "yes."

The Tao Of Silence

The Tao Of Silence